PLAINS ZEBRAS

by Lucia Raatma

Children's Press®

An Imprint of Scholastic Inc.
New York Toronto London Auckland Sydney
Mexico City New Delhi Hong Kong
Danbury, Connecticut

Content Consultant
Dr. Stephen S. Ditchkoff
Professor of Wildlife Sciences
Auburn University
Auburn, Alabama

Photographs © 2014: Alamy Images: 20, 21 (Photoshot Holdings Ltd), 18, 19 (Steve Bloom Images); Bob Italiano: 44 map, 45 map; Dreamstime: 2 background, 3 background, 44 background, 45 background (Annemario), 10, 11 (Kurt Nielsen), 35 (Mikle15), 6, 7 (Oleg Znamenskiy), 4, 5 background, 36, 37 (Stefanhuman), cover (Victor Soares); Getty Images/Heinrich van den Berg: 5 top inset, 15; iStockphoto/Paul Gregg: 28; Media Bakery/Christian Heinrich: 16, 17; Science Source/Roger Hall: 32, 33; Shutterstock, Inc.: 23 (Albie Venter), 1, 8, 9, 46 (maratr), 5 bottom inset, 40, 41 (Nadezhda1906); Superstock, Inc.: 12 (Charles Bowman), 30, 31 (imagebroker.net), 2 zebras, 3 zebras, 24, 25, 26, 27 (NHPA), 38, 39 (Ulrich Doering/imageb).

Library of Congress Cataloging-in-Publication Data
Raatma, Lucia, author.
 Plains zebras / by Lucia Raatma.
 pages cm. — (Nature's children)
 Summary: "This book details the life and habits of plains zebras." — Provided by publisher.
 Audience: 9–12.
 Audience: Grades 4 to 6.
 Includes bibliographical references and index.
 ISBN 978-0-531-21226-4 (lib. bdg.) — ISBN 978-0-531-25436-3 (pbk.)
 1. Burchell's zebra—Juvenile literature. 2. Zebras—Juvenile literature. I. Title. II. Series: Nature's children (New York, N.Y.)
 QL737.U62R33 2014
 599.665'7—dc23   2013019846

Printed in China 62
SCHOLASTIC, CHILDREN'S PRESS, and associated logos are trademarks and/or registered trademarks of Scholastic Inc.

1 2 3 4 5 6 7 8 9 10 R 23 22 21 20 19 18 17 16 15 14

Plains Zebras

Class	Mammalia
Order	Perissodactyla
Family	Equidae
Genus	*Equus*
Species	*Equus quagga*
World distribution	Many southern and eastern African countries, including Kenya, Tanzania, Namibia, Zambia, and Mozambique
Habitats	Primarily savannas, open woodlands, and areas of forest
Distinctive physical characteristics	Known for their thick black stripes; some have light brown "shadow" stripes as well; usually 47 to 55 inches (119 to 140 centimeters) tall; bodies are approximately 7.25 to 8.25 feet (2.2 to 2.5 meters) long; can weigh anywhere from 390 to 850 pounds (177 to 386 kilograms)
Habits	Live in groups called harems, which usually include one male and as many as six females, as well as their young; sometimes several harems group together to protect against predators
Diet	Mostly eat long and short grasses, leaves, and other vegetation

PLAINS ZEBRAS

Contents

CHAPTER 1

Stripes on the Savanna

It is a sunny day on the African **savanna**. A **harem** of plains zebras is feeding on grass. A group of wildebeests is **grazing** with them. Suddenly, the zebras hear a noise. They sense danger. Two hyenas dash out from the nearby trees and begin sprinting across the savanna toward the feeding animals. The zebra **stallion** races over to face the hyenas. He uses his mighty back legs to deliver a strong kick to one of the hyenas. Then he turns and bites at the other with his powerful jaws. The hyenas lunge at him, but he fights back with his front legs. Realizing they are outmatched, the hyenas turn and run back toward the trees.

The zebra stallion watches them go. Then he returns to the **mares** and young zebras he has protected. His actions have also helped the wildebeests. All of the animals return to their feeding. They can begin to calm down now that the danger has passed.

Members of a zebra harem stick together to help defend the group from threats.

The Zebra's Body

Plains zebras are **mammals**. They are also **ungulates**. This means they are animals that have **hooves** and that graze for food. Their bodies are long and muscular to help them run fast for long distances. Most zebras are 47 to 55 inches (119 to 140 centimeters) tall. Their bodies are approximately 7.25 to 8.25 feet (2.2 to 2.5 meters) long. Plains zebras can weigh anywhere from 390 to 850 pounds (177 to 386 kilograms). Males and females are often the same size.

A mane extends from the top of a zebra's head along the back of its neck. The black-and-white hair in the mane stands straight up. At the other end of the zebra's body is a narrow tail. The tail is usually 18.5 to 22 inches (47 to 56 cm) long, with a fluffy black tuft of hair at the end.

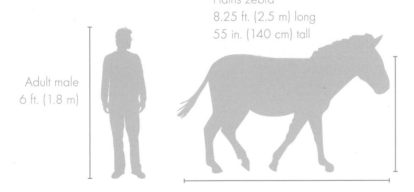

Plains zebra
8.25 ft. (2.5 m) long
55 in. (140 cm) tall

Adult male
6 ft. (1.8 m)

The stripes on a zebra's mane match up with the stripes on its body.

Black and White

A plains zebra's body is covered in thick black-and-white stripes that are widely spaced apart. Some zebras have lighter "shadow" stripes in between the black ones. The plains zebra's stripes are arranged vertically on the main part of the body. They are arranged horizontally on the animal's hind parts. A zebra's stripes are like a human's fingerprints. No two zebras have patterns that are exactly alike.

Scientists have different ideas about why zebras have stripes. Some think the stripes help hide zebras from **predators**. When predators try to attack a group of zebras, the stripes make it hard for the predators to single out one animal. Instead, they see a mass of crisscrossing stripes. This might cause them to pause for a split second, giving the zebras time to scramble away.

Some think the stripes help keep a zebra's body at just the right temperature. Others think the stripes help keep horseflies from landing on the zebras' bodies and biting them. Because the stripe patterns are all different, they might also help zebras recognize one another.

A plains zebra's shadow stripes are sometimes difficult to see.

Where Zebras Live

The plains zebra is the most common **species** of **equid** in the world. There are about 750,000 of these incredible animals roaming throughout a variety of natural **habitats** today. They spend most of their time in savannas, woodlands, and forested areas. Most zebra habitats are located at sea level. However, some zebras live high up on the grassy areas of Mount Kenya, the second-tallest mountain in Africa. These zebras are found at elevations of up to 14,100 feet (4,300 m) above sea level.

Plains zebras also occupy a wider range of land than any other equid species. Most plains zebras are found in the southern and eastern parts of Africa. They live as far north as the southern portions of Sudan and Ethiopia and as far south as Zambia, Mozambique, and northern Zimbabwe.

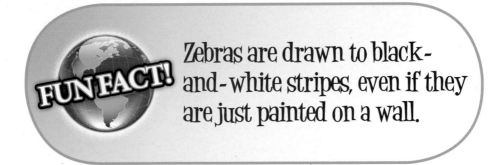

FUN FACT! Zebras are drawn to black-and-white stripes, even if they are just painted on a wall.

Some zebras live in the area near Mount Kilimanjaro, in Kenya.

CHAPTER 2

Surviving in Africa

Zebras spend almost all of their time finding and eating food. On an average day, a plains zebra might spend as many as 18 hours feeding. Plains zebras are **herbivores**. They graze on a variety of grasses and other plants, including herbs and shrubs. Zebras eat more than the green leaves of these plants. They also feed on the stems and roots. They even eat twigs and bark.

Zebras have strong front teeth to help them eat all of these plant parts. As a plains zebra grazes, it uses these teeth to bite off pieces of food. It then uses its flat back teeth to crush and grind the food. A zebra's teeth slowly wear down because of the constant feeding and chewing.

Zebras move their jaws from side to side to grind up mouthfuls of grass and other plant parts.

Equipped for Their Environment

The plants that zebras eat have very low levels of the **nutrients** that the animals need to live. Other ungulates would not be able to survive if they followed a zebra's diet. However, zebras' bodies are designed to **digest** the plants quickly. This allows the zebras to eat more food than their relatives can. Even though each bite of food has fewer nutrients, a zebra eats so much that it still gets the nutrition its body needs.

Zebras sometimes need to **migrate** to find food and water. The land in Africa can be rugged and dry. The zebras need water to survive. They drink it often, so they tend to live close to lakes or watering holes. They also need rain so that the plants they eat can grow. When an area gets too dry, a group of zebras might travel hundreds of miles in search of water.

Zebras sometimes wade into pools of water to drink.

On the Lookout

There are many dangerous predators in the wilds of Africa. Plains zebras must watch out for enemies. Their main predators are lions and hyenas. They also have to be careful of leopards and wild dogs. When zebras are traveling near rivers, Nile crocodiles are another threat.

All day and night, zebras have to be careful. Their **foals** are especially weak when attacked by larger, stronger animals. At night, plains zebras often stay in wide-open areas. This way, they can more easily spot approaching predators.

Plains zebras have strong senses that help them notice nearby predators before it is too late. They have especially powerful hearing and vision. Because their eyes are located on the sides of their heads, zebras can see all around them. They can also see very well at night.

Open areas give zebras plenty of time to spot approaching predators and escape before they are attacked.

Powerful Protectors

When predators attack, it is up to the stallions to protect females and younger zebras. They also help protect any harem members that are wounded. The stallions are strong fighters. They can defend against small groups of predators such as hyenas. They can even fight off lion attacks. In fact, zebras can be so fierce that lions usually have to work together to hunt them. Zebras' legs deliver powerful kicks. Also, zebras group together and form circles around predators and bite at them with their strong jaws.

To stay safe, plains zebras may also join together with other animals. Harems of zebras may join groups of wildebeests, ostriches, antelopes, and giraffes. The different animals can sense when others are aware of danger. This makes it easier for them to notice threats and flee to safety. These mixed groups can be made up of hundreds and hundreds of animals.

FUN FACT! A zebra's kick is powerful enough to kill a lion in one hit.

Zebra stallions are not afraid to fight lions and other predators head-to-head.

CHAPTER 3

A Zebra's Life

A plains zebra harem usually consists of one stallion and several mares. The stallion **mates** with all of the mares in the group. All of the foals produced by the harem's mares also become part of the group. Sometimes the mares are not friendly with one another. The stallion must protect mares that are new to the group. Sometimes a male zebra from outside the group may try to join the harem. He must first challenge the harem's stallion for control of the group. The two zebras fight each other to prove their strength. They strike each other with powerful kicks and bites. If the outside male wins the fight, the other stallion leaves the group. However, the outsider will back away if he loses. Usually, these outsiders live in groups with other males who are older or have been unable to gain control of a harem.

Male zebras do battle by biting at each other's necks and attempting to wrestle the other to the ground.

Sending Signals

Zebras communicate using a variety of body language and sounds. For example, a zebra's ears stand up straight when the zebra is calm or friendly. When it is scared, its ears seem pushed forward. If its ears are pushed back, that means the zebra is angry.

Members of a harem will frequently **groom** one another. Mares and foals do this most often. They use their lips and teeth to nip others at their neck, shoulders, and back. Brothers and sisters may groom each other, too. Scientists believe that grooming helps the zebras grow closer. It may also help them calm down after a threat has passed.

Zebras can be very noisy. Mares make a whining sound if they lose sight of their young. They make a neighing sound called a nicker if they sense danger. Zebras often make yelping sounds to warn others of a nearby predator.

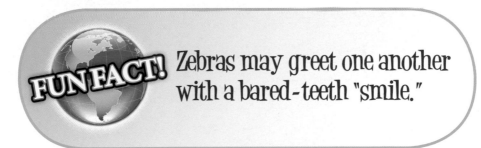

FUN FACT! Zebras may greet one another with a bared-teeth "smile."

Zebras often strengthen relationships with fellow harem members by grooming each other.

Zebra Mating

Male and female zebras can mate any time of year. However, plains zebras are most likely to mate during the rainy season. After mating, the mare is pregnant for 12 to 13 months before it is time to give birth. A zebra mare usually gives birth to just one foal at a time. However, in rare cases, she may have twins. A mare can get pregnant again very soon after giving birth. This means she can have a foal almost once a year.

When a foal is born, it weighs about 70 pounds (32 kg). It can stand up on its own almost as soon as it is born. It learns to walk and run within just a day. At first, the young zebra survives by drinking milk from its mother. It learns to graze for food within a week or so of birth. In addition to grazing, it continues to drink its mother's milk until it is 13 to 16 months old. In order to avoid danger, the young zebra stays very close to its older relatives until it is large and strong enough to defend itself.

Newborn zebra foals look like tiny versions of their parents.

Out on Their Own

About half of all wild zebra foals live to be adults. Those that do not survive are often victims of lion or hyena attacks. Young zebras stay with their mother's harem until they are between one and three years old. At that point, young male zebras leave the harem to join groups of other males.

Male zebras are ready to begin mating and producing foals of their own when they are about four years old. To do so, they must form their own harems with young female zebras. Female zebras can start mating when they are between two and four years old. Males compete to add these young females to their harems.

In the wild, zebras often live to be 20 to 25 years old. Those that live in zoos and wildlife parks, where there are few threats, can live to be 40 years old.

FUN FACT! Zebras bathe using dust or mud. As they shake off the dirt, it removes loose hair and skin.

Young stallions often group together until they can take over a harem or form harems of their own.

CHAPTER 4

Zebras Then and Now

In addition to the plains zebra, there are two other zebra species living today. The mountain zebra lives in southern and southwestern Africa, in such countries as Angola, Namibia, and South Africa. It looks much like a plains zebra, but its stripes are narrower and its belly is white.

The Grevy's zebra has the narrowest stripes of all three species. It has a white belly and a long black stripe that runs along its back from head to tail. This species is found almost exclusively in the nation of Kenya.

Both the Grevy's zebra and the mountain zebra are far less common than the plains zebra. While there are hundreds of thousands of plains zebras roaming throughout a large part of Africa, there are only about 2,500 Grevy's zebras and 1,400 to 2,000 mountain zebras living today.

A Grevy's zebra's thin stripes come in different patterns than those of other zebra species.

Ancient Equids

Scientists believe that zebras first appeared within the last 4 million years. However, their earliest equid ancestors roamed the earth somewhere between 56 million and 34 million years ago.

One way scientists learn about ancient equids and other **extinct** species is by studying **fossils**. Fossils of ancient equids have been found all over the world. In fact, they have been found on every **continent** except for Australia and Antarctica.

In the 1920s and 1930s, a large discovery of fossils was made at the Hagerman Fossil Beds in Hagerman, Idaho. Among other discoveries, scientists found hundreds of fossils of an ancient horse species. They called this extinct species the Hagerman horse. It is considered the world's first true equid species. All of today's zebras, donkeys, and horses are related to this ancient horse.

The Hagerman horse is one of the plains zebra's earliest ancestors.

Equid Cousins

Aside from zebras, there are two other types of equids living today. One type is the horse. Horses look very much like zebras. Both have four strong legs with hooves. Their heads have similar shapes. Their ears and teeth are similar, too. The most obvious difference between them is that horses lack zebras' distinctive black-and-white-striped pattern. Also, the hair in a horse's mane usually lays flat instead of sticking straight up. Most horses are **domestic**. People ride them and use them to help with work on farms. However, there are also some wild horses living in certain parts of the world today.

The other group of modern equids is made up of the donkey and the wild ass. These two species are very similar to each other. The main difference between them is that donkeys are domesticated and wild asses are not. These equids are much smaller and slower than horses or zebras.

Horses are often bred and trained to participate in races.

CHAPTER 5

What's Next?

Unlike many other wild animals in Africa, plains zebras are not **endangered**. However, there are fewer plains zebras today than in years past. Habitat loss is one of the biggest causes of the shrinking zebra population. The human population is getting larger and larger. This means villages and towns must expand to make more room for buildings, farms, and roads. This leaves less space for the zebras to graze. In addition, zebras rely on certain paths to migrate and follow the rainy weather. When these paths are ruined, the zebras have difficulty getting the water and food they need.

Illegal hunting is another reason there are fewer zebras today. Some hunters kill zebras for their meat. Others want to sell their unique striped skins. These skins are worth a great deal of money on the black market.

Habitat destruction leaves zebras and other animals with less space to roam and less food to eat.

Important Animals

Throughout Africa, zebras provide many benefits for people. They are beautiful animals that tourists enjoy watching. Zebras help improve tourism, which brings needed money to the countries of Africa. People from all over the world like to travel to Africa for **safaris**. They hope to see zebras and other interesting animals in the wild. **Ecotourism** provides jobs for people who work in hotels and restaurants. It also provides jobs for drivers and tour guides.

In addition, zebras play an important role in the **ecosystem**. They eat plants that other animals do not want. They eat old growth and stems, which makes way for new grasses to grow. Zebras also kick up dirt when they migrate during the rainy season. This helps prepare the ground for plants to grow. Other animals, such as wildebeests and antelopes, feed on the newly grown plants.

Some tourists travel deep into the wild regions of Africa to glimpse at zebras and other animals in their natural setting.

Protecting Zebras

Even though plains zebras are not in danger of dying out soon, their numbers are decreasing. Many people are working to ensure that zebra populations do not get even smaller. Throughout Africa, plains zebras live in wildlife **preserves**. Among these are Kruger National Park in South Africa, Hwange National Park in Zimbabwe, and Serengeti National Park in Tanzania. Zebras in such areas are safe from hunters and other dangers.

Zebras also live in zoos and animal parks in countries around the world. Zookeepers try to re-create the zebras' natural habitat. They feed them the same grasses and leaves that the animals would eat in the wild. Visitors to the parks are able to learn about zebras and how they live. With programs like these, we can help spread the word about zebras and make sure that these beautiful animals continue to live healthy lives in their natural habitats.

Zoos are a great way to get a close look at zebras.

Words to Know

continent (KAHN-tuh-nuhnt) — one of seven large landmasses on the earth; they are Asia, Africa, Europe, North America, South America, Australia, and Antarctica

digest (dye-JEST) — to break down food into forms that can be taken in and used by the body

domestic (duh-MES-tik) — animals that have been tamed; people use them as a source of food or as work animals, or keep them as pets

ecosystem (EE-koh-sis-tuhm) — all the living things in a place and their relation to the environment

ecotourism (ee-koh-TUR-iz-uhm) — business that focuses on helping travelers learn about the environment

endangered (en-DAYN-jurd) — at risk of becoming extinct, usually because of human activity

equid (EH-kwid) — an animal belonging to the genus *Equus*

extinct (ik-STINGKT) — no longer found alive; known about only through fossils or history

foals (FOHLZ) — young zebras, horses, mules, or donkeys

fossils (FAH-suhlz) — bones, shells, or other traces of an animal or plant from long ago, preserved as rock

grazing (GRAY-zing) — feeding on grass that is growing in a field

groom (GROOM) — to clean and maintain the appearance of an animal

habitats (HAB-uh-tats) — the places where an animal or a plant naturally lives

harem (HARE-uhm) — a group of zebras consisting of one male, several females, and their young

herbivores (HUR-buh-vorz) — animals that eat only plants

hooves (HOOVZ) — the hard parts that cover the feet of animals such as zebras and deer

mammals (MAM-uhlz) — warm-blooded animals that have hair or fur and usually give birth to live young

mares (MAIRZ) — female zebras, horses, or donkeys

mates (MAYTZ) — joins together to produce babies

migrate (MYE-grate) — to move to another area or climate at a particular time of year

nutrients (NOO-tree-uhnts) — substances such as protein, minerals, and vitamins that are needed by people, animals, and plants to stay strong and healthy

predators (PRED-uh-turz) — animals that live by hunting other animals for food

preserves (pri-ZURVZ) — places where animals and plants are protected in their natural environment

safaris (suh-FAHR-eez) — trips taken, usually to Africa, to see or hunt large wild animals

savanna (suh-VAN-uh) — a flat, grassy plain with few or no trees

species (SPEE-sheez) — one of the groups into which animals and plants of the same genus are divided; members of the same species can mate and have offspring

stallion (STAL-yuhn) — an adult male zebra or horse

ungulates (UN-gyuh-luts) — mammals that have hooves and graze for food

Habitat Map

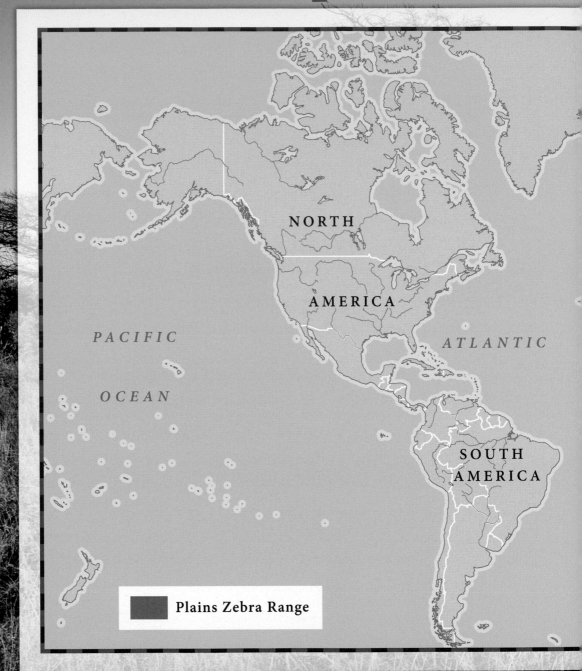

NORTH

AMERICA

PACIFIC

OCEAN

ATLANTIC

SOUTH

AMERICA

Plains Zebra Range

ARCTIC OCEAN

EUROPE

ASIA

AFRICA

PACIFIC
OCEAN

INDIAN

OCEAN

OCEAN

AUSTRALIA

Find Out More

Books

Friedman, Mel. *Africa*. New York: Children's Press, 2009.

Stewart, Melissa. *Zebras*. New York: Children's Press, 2002.

Stone, Lynn M. *Zebras*. Minneapolis: Lerner Publications, 2009.

Visit this Scholastic Web site for more information on plains zebras:
www.factsfornow.scholastic.com
Enter the keywords **Plains Zebras**

Index

Page numbers in *italics* indicate a photograph or map.

About the Author

Lucia Raatma earned a bachelor's degree from the University of South Carolina and a master's degree from New York University. She has authored dozens of books for young readers, and she particularly enjoys writing about wildlife and conservation. She and her family love watching the zebras at the local wildlife park.